D1355788

The
Fireside Book

A picture and a poem
for every mood
chosen by

David Hope

Printed and Published by
D. C. THOMSON & CO. LTD.,
185 Fleet Street, London EC4A 2HS.
© D. C. Thomson & Co. Ltd., 1985.
ISBN 0 85116 343 2

CONTRASTS

MY stately lady from the town wears silken hose and silken gown.

Her lips are red as any rose, but not of nature, heaven knows.

Not a hair is out of place, and there is powder on her face.

In fact, though rumoured rather naughty,

She's cold and proud and much too haughty.

But Julie wears a simple dress that suits her lissome
  loveliness.
Her lips are full and very sweet, and always
  smiling when we meet.
Her hair oft tumbles o'er her eyes, but they are
  blue as summer skies.
The lady's not for me, that's plain;
So I'll kiss Julie in the lane.

Peter Cliffe

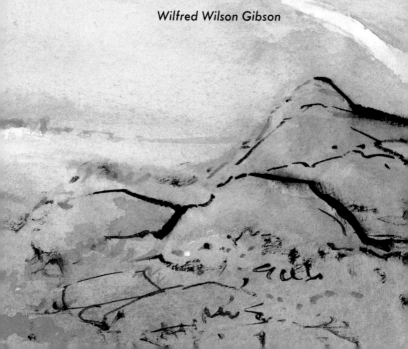

BY MOONLIGHT

THE night we took the bees out to the heather,
   The sealed hives stacked behind us, as
   together
We rode in the jingly jolting cart, were humming
Like the far-murmuring rumour of blown branches.

White in the moon-flame was the flowering
   heather
And white the sandy trackway, as together
We travelled, and a dewy scent of honey
Hung in the warm, white, windless air of midnight.

A silvery trackway through moon-silvered heather
To the humming dark of the hives, we'll ride
   together
For evermore through murmurous dewy midnight,
My heart, a hive of honey-scented moonlight.

Wilfred Wilson Gibson

SMITH SQUARE

IN Smith Square, Westminster, the houses stand so prim;
  With slender railings at their feet and windows straight
    and slim;
And all day long they staidly stare with gentle, placid
  gaze,
And dream of joyous happenings in splendid bygone days.

In Smith Square, Westminster, you must not make a noise,
No shrill-voiced vendors harbour there, no shouting errand-
  boys;
But very busy gentlemen step swiftly out and in,
With little leather cases and umbrellas neatly thin.

Yet sometimes when the summer night her starry curtain
  spreads,
And all the busy gentlemen are sleeping in their beds,
You hear a gentle humming like the humming of a hive,
And Smith Square, Westminster, begins to come alive.

For all the houses start to sing, honey-sweet and low,
The little tender lovely songs of long and long ago,
And all the fairies round about come hastening up in
  crowds,
Until the quiet air is filled with rainbow-coloured clouds.

And long before the butlers stumble drowsily downstairs,
And long before their masters have begun to say their
  prayers,
The fairies all have pranced away upon the morning
  beams,
And Smith Square, Westminster, is wrapped once more in
  dreams.

Rose Fyleman

MY LOVE

OH, let the snowflakes nestle
    So lightly in your hair
As if the wind had won you
    Jewels from the air
And brought them now by hundreds
    To glitter in your hair.

And let your hair go flying
    About your cheeks and eyes
To veil them so a moment,
    Then again surprise
With all the sudden beauty
    Of your uncovered eyes.

John Buxton

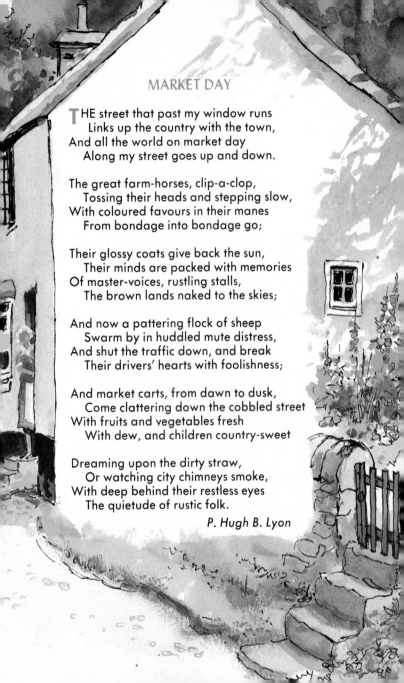

MARKET DAY

THE street that past my window runs
  Links up the country with the town,
And all the world on market day
  Along my street goes up and down.

The great farm-horses, clip-a-clop,
  Tossing their heads and stepping slow,
With coloured favours in their manes
  From bondage into bondage go;

Their glossy coats give back the sun,
  Their minds are packed with memories
Of master-voices, rustling stalls,
  The brown lands naked to the skies;

And now a pattering flock of sheep
  Swarm by in huddled mute distress,
And shut the traffic down, and break
  Their drivers' hearts with foolishness;

And market carts, from dawn to dusk,
  Come clattering down the cobbled street
With fruits and vegetables fresh
  With dew, and children country-sweet

Dreaming upon the dirty straw,
  Or watching city chimneys smoke,
With deep behind their restless eyes
  The quietude of rustic folk.

P. Hugh B. Lyon

AT DAWN

I KNOW a dingle in a leafy wood
   Filled with the fragrance of the perfect May.
Here the grey trees for centuries have stood,
   And Spring wreathes garlands on them, new
      and gay.
Is there a moment of the shining day,
   Fairer than this, which sees the rising sun
Slant the pale yellow of his early ray
   On dew-drenched fallows, and the fine
      threads spun
By long-legged spinners in the clefts of trees,
Float their light gossamer upon the breeze?
Here leaps the limber-footed, listening hare—
And here the cuckoo, blithe and debonair,
   Calls from the willows in the water leas,
Remote, elusive, a thin tongue of air.

Pamela Tennant

SOME MUST WORK...

THE world is planned in such a way
    That some must work and some must play:
Each one of us should strive, with zest,
To do the thing that suits him best.

While I adore the dappled shade
By the light, quivering aspen made,
(*I quote*) My wife prefers to hoe,
Or plant potatoes in a row.

So, while I spend exhausting hours
In eating plums and smelling flowers,
My wife, true daughter of the soil,
Delights in her delicious toil.

                        Reginald Arkell

THE TAMIL MAID

WHERE through the jungle's shade
    Men's feet a path have made,
Comes a tall Tamil maid
    Sauntering slow!

In her red *Sele* dressed
Lightly the grass she pressed,
And the glad leaves caressed
    Each little toe.

Twined is her long black hair
On neck and shoulders bare;
Her ears and ankles rare
    Gaily bedight.

Sunlight her bosom warms
Glancing athwart her charms;
Bangles upon her arms
    Shine silver-bright.

Brown are her lovely eyes,
Lit with a sweet surprise,
Deep as the shadow lies
    Under the sea.

Teeth like the dews of morn
Blithely her lips adorn,
Lips with a look half scorn,
    Peerless and free.

E. C. Dumbleton

ROADS

THOSE Roman roads are not for me
    That march direct from A to B.
How bold they are, with all revealed;
No curve or slope to hold concealed
A sudden glimpse of poppies gay
Or distant castle, ruined, grey;
But single-minded, stern and straight.
Left right! Quick march! No time to wait!

Give me instead the winding way
By streams where willows droop and sway
With flash of feather in between;
A hump-backed bridge on which to lean.
Our forebears, travelling around
The line of least resistance found
And cared not if a passing crow
Showed them a swifter way to go.

To those who once, with feet roughshod,
The countryside in silence trod,
My thanks for paths which curve and bend
And keep their secrets to the end.

Silvie Taylor

THE FISHER

THE fisher stood beside the stream
  And heard the water gurgling by;
Life for a moment was a dream,
And time a tiny pebble's sigh.

He flicked his line; it lightly fell
Upstream a bit, then drifted down;
Thus, patiently he plied his skill
Until the setting of the sun.

Then over stile and thistle-top,
Content, he made his way to town;
And safely settled on his cap,
His chosen fly—the small March-brown!

Edward Borland Ramsay

THE SUSSEX DOWNS

I PRESS my cheek against thyme-scented grass
   Where wind-tossed clouds in gay processional
Lean overhead and watch me as they go.
   Here can I lie with outstretched arms and hear
The throbbing music of the mounting lark,
   And near-by hum of honey-laden bees.
And gazing sleepily through half-closed lids
   I see bare hills and vales of folded peace,
Where massy elms like brooding sentinels
   Lean over gabled farmsteads drowsing through
Heat-hazy noons and clover-scented dawns.

Florence Irene Gubbins

THE TOLL-GATE HOUSE

THE toll-gate's gone, but still stands lone,
 In the dip of the hill, the house of stone,
And over the roof in the branching pine
The great owl sits in the white moonshine.
An old man lives, and lonely, there,
His windows yet on the cross-roads stare,
And on Michaelmas night in all the years
A galloping far and faint he hears . . .
His casement open wide he flings
With " Who goes there?" and a lantern swings . . .
But never more in the dim moonbeam
Than a cloak and a plume and the silver gleam
Of passing spurs in the night can he see,
For the toll-gate's gone and the road is free.

John Drinkwater

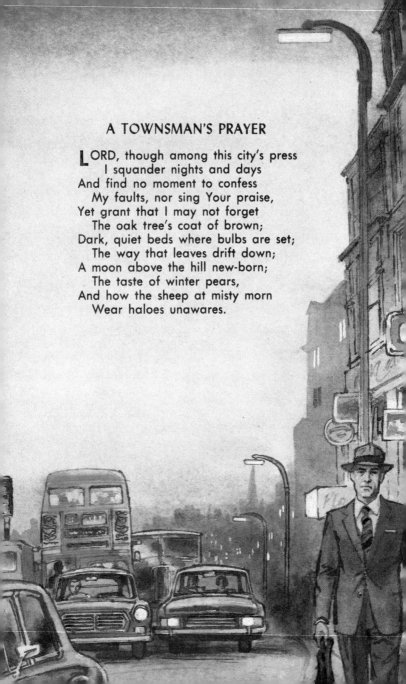

A TOWNSMAN'S PRAYER

LORD, though among this city's press
   I squander nights and days
And find no moment to confess
   My faults, nor sing Your praise,
Yet grant that I may not forget
   The oak tree's coat of brown;
Dark, quiet beds where bulbs are set;
   The way that leaves drift down;
A moon above the hill new-born;
   The taste of winter pears,
And how the sheep at misty morn
   Wear haloes unawares.

The last-left apple's wrinkled cheek
  Where high and free it swings;
The way that country people speak;
  A magpie's mottled wings.
Take my wild heart and strip it bare
  And teach me to be wise
Who have loved nothing, Lord, more fair
  Than winter skies.

Eiluned Lewis

HANDS

TEMPEST without; within, the mellow glow
   Of mingling lamp and firelight over all—
Etchings and watercolours on the wall,
Cushions and curtains of clear indigo,
Rugs, damask-red and blue as Tyrian seas,
Deep chairs, black oaken settles, hammered brass,
Translucent porcelain and sea-green glass—
Colour and warmth and light and dreamy ease.

And I sit wondering where are now the hands
That wrought at anvil, easel, wheel and loom—
Hands, slender, swart, red, gnarled—in foreign
   lands
Or English shops to furnish this seemly room;
And all the while, without, the windy rain
Drums like dead fingers tapping at the pane.

Wilfred Wilson Gibson

CAPRICE

DAISY, daisy, daisy sweet,
　　Tell me, if you can,
When, if ever, I shall meet
My fine gentleman.

Daisy, daisy, tell me, do,
Tell me, if you will,
Is my lover fond and true?
Does he love me still?

Daisy, daisy, daisy, pray,
If you can then tell
What your pretty petals say,
Does he love me well?

He loves me; he loves me not.
Daisy! Is this so?
Have I been by him forgot?
How can petals know?

Ah! he loves me yet again,
Oh! he loves me never,
Ah, he loves me and, 'tis plain,
He will love me ever.

Daisy petals, blowing free,
Sudden is my whim,
Tell the gentleman for me
That I don't love him!

Sam MacEachan

THE WORLD DISCOVERED

IT is enough that sea and air,
   This summer morn,
And hills and trees should sweetly wear
   A look new-born;
The very cows that stand about,
   Their horns fresh curled,
From Noah's ark have just come out
   To view the world.

And when I find, like pigeon's wing,
   Sea-lavender along the shore,
I'll stoop to pick the pretty thing
   And ask for nothing more.

Eiluned Lewis

THE RUSHES

THE rushes nod by the river
   As the winds on the loud waves go,
And the things they nod of are many,
For it's many the secret they know.

And I think they are wise as the fairies
Who lived ere the hills were high,
They nod so grave by the river
To everyone passing by.

If they would tell me their secrets
I would go by a hidden way,
To the rath when the moon retiring
Dips dim horns into the gray.

And a fairy-girl out of Leinster
In a long dance I should meet,
My heart to her heart beating,
My feet in rhyme with her feet.

                        Francis Ledwidge

A JUNE BIRTHDAY

THERE'S the lark, my dear, and the blackbird, and
   all the beautiful throng,
Madder and merrier now than ever they've been
   the whole year yet,
Fiddle and fife and reedy flute in their shrill,
   ecstatic song;
For it's June, my dear, and your birthday, and
   Summer cannot forget.

The sun has been over the tree-tops this long, long
   hour and more,
And the wind's like a morris-dancer, stepping out
   to the blackbird's flute,
And little whispering leaf-shadows creep in to
   dance on your floor—
Oh, lean from your window and listen to us, for
   never a singer is mute!

                    Thora Stowell

ODE TO MARCH

OH, March, you roar around our house,
    Your laden skies are black,
You whistle down our chimney pot,
    And play games in the stack.
The sudden, squally, wind-tossed showers,
    Soak washing on my line,
Then fly as quickly as they came,
    And soon the day is fine.
The ragged clouds are blown along
    Across a steely sky,
And in and out our letter box,
    You come to peek and pry.
Oh, March, please tell me why it is,
    You make this fearful noise?
I think you must be jealous
    Of sweet April's Springtime joys.
We wait for April patiently,
    As wild trees bend and sway,
And hope that all your bullying
    Won't blow her clean away!

Susan Benwell

THE PEDLAR'S CARAVAN

I WISH I lived in a caravan
   With a horse to drive like a pedlar-man!
Where he comes from nobody knows,
Or where he goes to, but on he goes!

His caravan has windows two,
And a chimney of tin that the smoke comes
   through;
He has a wife, with a baby brown,
And they go riding from tòwn to town.

Chairs to mend, and delf to sell!
He clashes the basins like a bell;
Tea-trays, baskets ranged in order,
Plates with alphabets round the border!

With the pedlar-man I should like to roam,
And write a book when I came home;
All the people would read my book,
Just like the travels of Captain Cook!

William Brighty Rands

THE CURIO SHOP

CURIOS, curios, row upon row,
　　Small ones above, tall ones below;
Pieces of china, old as can be,
Odd cups and saucers, a quaint pot for tea.

Elegant figures, all dressed so fine,
Crystal glass goblets for ruby red wine;
Small clocks and watches in a glass case,
Measuring out their slow, steady pace.

Large copper kettles shining so bright,
Oval gilt mirrors reflecting the light;
Lacquered snuff boxes from distant Japan,
Occasional tables from the reign of Queen Anne.

Once they had owners to tend them with care,
To dust down that vase and polish that chair;
They gazed in the mirror and ate from this plate,
Never once guessing what would be its fate.

Almost I hear them whispering to me,
" Please take it home, for can you not see,
These things were loved—it's what makes them
　　glow—
They will give back all the love you bestow."

And so I choose—a candlestick bright
That twinkles and gleams as it catches the light,
And as I leave, I hear a voice say,
" You're lucky, you've found a new friend today!"

Glenda Moore

ORCHARDS

SOMETIMES, in apple country, you may see
  A ghostly orchard standing all in white,
Aisles of white trees, white branches, in the green,
On some still day when the year hangs between
Winter and spring, and heaven is full of light.
And rising from the ground pale clouds of smoke
Float through the trees and hang upon the air,
Trailing their wisps of blue like a swelled cloak
From the round cheeks of breezes. But though fair
To him who leans upon the gate to stare
And muse " How delicate in spring they be,
That mobled blossom and that wimpled tree,"
There is a purpose in the cloudy aisles
That took no thought of beauty for its care.
For here's the beauty of all country miles,
Their rolling pattern and their space:
That there's a reason for each changing square,
Here sleeping fallow, there a meadow mown,
All to their use ranged different each year,
The shaven grass, the gold, the brindled roan,
Not in some search for empty grace,
But fine through service and intent sincere.

Victoria Sackville-West

COME IN

COME in from the dark night,
  Shut fast the door;
I have kept the lamp alight
  And swept the floor,
And put away from sight
  What passed before.

Be still; rest and forget;
  This hour redeems
The long day's toil and fret;
  The firelight gleams
Where dusk and silence set
  A trap for dreams.

Your tired head resting, so,
  Beneath my hand,
For a little while we'll go
  In twilight land,
Silent, because you know
  I understand.

F. Y. Walters

PASSING FANCIES

WHEN I was just turned seventeen
    I fell in love with Alice Green;
And oh, but I was very sure
That she'd be mine for evermore.

When I was nearly twenty-one
I set my cap at Sarah Dunn;
And thought that love had come to stay,
But someone stole her heart away.

When I was touching twenty-three
I had a kiss from Paula Lee;
And I became her constant swain,
Until she fell in love again.

Now here I am at thirty-two,
And very glad I married Pru,
Because she's sweet and so much fun;
But what have all the others done?

Well, Alice shares a farmer's life,
And Sarah is a vicar's wife;
Paula's found a millionaire,
But I've got Pru—so I don't care!

Peter Cliffe

LOVERS' MEETING

WHEN all alone, my love I frame
In courtly phrase or gay conceit,
And make a music of her name
To charm her when we meet.

But when I stand before her face,
My heart such sweet diversion brings,
That words are scattered out of place
In feeble stammerings.

How faint and weak must I appear,
Who hold my life at her command!
Stoop, Love, and whisper in her ear,
That she may understand.

P. Hugh B. Lyon

EVERY HOUR A SONG

O TO lie a-dreaming
  In the heather by the sea,
And watch the sapphires gleaming
In the waters of Tiree;
To hear the white waves singing
Like the heart-beat of an oar,
While the gulls are gaily winging
By the cockle shore.

O to be a-tramping
When the sun is in the west,
To hear the mellow lilting
Of the lochan's sleepy crest;
To think a while and tarry
In the evening when it's still,
With no tempting thought to hurry
Round the lonely hill.

O to lie a-dreaming
When the moon is in the sky,
To watch the pale stars leaming
While the cares of life go by;
To know that in our living
All our brighter joys belong
To the happy gift of giving
Every hour a song.

Edward Borland Ramsay

FOR THIS AND MORE

FOR all your patient care;
    For every anguished prayer;
For every gentle look;
For every step you took;
For every anxious night;
For every kindly light;
For tact with awkward ways;
For love on wayward days;
For hope when there was none;
For faith when hope was done;
For all you ever thought;
For all you ever wrought;
Today, and now, and here,
I thank you, mother dear.

Fay Inchfawn

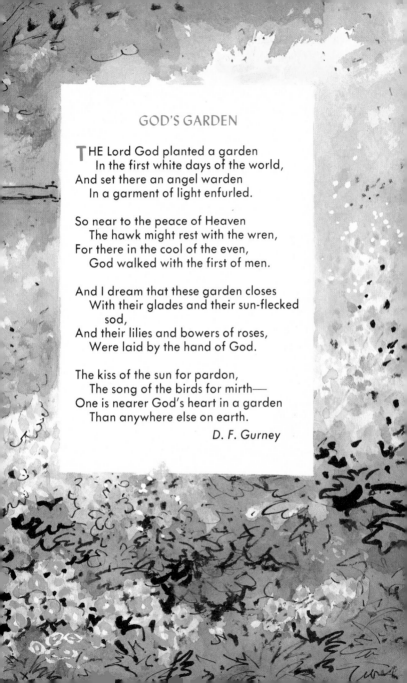

GOD'S GARDEN

THE Lord God planted a garden
   In the first white days of the world,
And set there an angel warden
   In a garment of light enfurled.

So near to the peace of Heaven
   The hawk might rest with the wren,
For there in the cool of the even,
   God walked with the first of men.

And I dream that these garden closes
   With their glades and their sun-flecked
      sod,
And their lilies and bowers of roses,
   Were laid by the hand of God.

The kiss of the sun for pardon,
   The song of the birds for mirth—
One is nearer God's heart in a garden
   Than anywhere else on earth.

D. F. Gurney

LAD'S LOVE

IF you have me for sweetheart and I have you for
  dear,
There's little left for longing and little left to fear;
The hungry winds will wander, the hungry seas will
  cry,
But we shall cease from hunger and let sad
  thoughts go by.

The winds must leave the waters, the stars must
  leave the night,
Ere we be done with loving or put away delight;
The dawns shall all be golden, the skies shall all be
  clear,
If you have me for sweetheart and I have you for
  dear.

Gerald Gould

A MARCH DAY

THE cock is crowing,
   The stream is flowing,
   The small birds twitter,
   The lake doth glitter,
The green field sleeps in the sun;
   The oldest and youngest
   Are at work with the strongest;
   The cattle are grazing,
   Their heads never raising;
There are forty feeding like one!

   Like an army defeated
   The snow hath retreated,
   And now doth fare ill
   On the top of the bare hill;
The ploughboy is whooping-anon-anon;
   There's joy in the mountains;
   There's life in the fountains;
   Small clouds are sailing:
   Blue sky prevailing;
The rain is over and gone!

William Wordsworth

THE PAISLEY SHAWL

WHAT were his dreams who wove this coloured
   shawl—
The grey, hard-bitten weaver, gaunt and dour,
Out of whose grizzled memory, even as a flower
Out of bleak Winter at young April's call
In the old tradition of flowers breaks into bloom,
Blossomed the ancient intricate design
Of softly-glowing hues and exquisite line—
What were his dreams, crouched at his cottage-
   loom?

What were *her* dreams, the laughing April lass,
   Who first, in the flower of young delight
With parted lips and eager tilted head
   And shining eyes, about her shoulders white
Drew the soft fabric of kindling green and red,
Standing before the candle-lighted glass?

Wilfred Wilson Gibson

I HEARD A LINNET

I HEARD a linnet courting
    His lady in the Spring:
His mates were idly sporting,
    Nor stayed to hear him sing
        His song of love—
I fear my speech distorting
    His tender love.

The phrases of his pleading
    Were full of young delight:
And she that gave him heeding
    Interpreted aright
        His gay, sweet notes—
So sadly marred in the reading—
    His tender notes.

And when he ceased, the hearer
    Awaited the refrain,
Till swiftly perching nearer
    He sang his song again,
        His pretty song:—
Would that my verse spake clearer
    His tender song!

Ye happy, airy creatures!
    That in the merry Spring
Think not of what misfeatures
    Or cares the year may bring;
        But unto love
Resign your simple natures,
    To tender love.

Robert Bridges

THE APPLE TREES

THERE are five apple trees here, standing in a
   row:
One day, when the wind began to blow,
   I watched the petals falling
      Into the ditch below.

Beyond the wire is an orchard full of apple trees;
One morning the petals fallen from these
   Were lying thickly strewn
      Over the grass below.

In my garden in England an apple tree stands;
Today the petals are fluttering over her hands
   While she is gathering the bluebells
      And the celandines below.

John Buxton

LONDON TOWN

OH, London Town's a fine town, and London sights are
   rare,
And London ale is right ale, and brisk's the London air,
And busily goes the world there, but crafty grows the
   mind,
And London Town, of all towns, I'm glad to leave
   behind.

Then hey for croft and hop-yard, and hill, and field, and
   pond,
With Bredon Hill before me and Malvern Hill beyond,
The hawthorn white i' the hedgerow, and all the spring's
   attire
In the comely land of Teme and Lugg, and Clent, and
   Clee, and Wyre.

Oh London girls are brave girls, in silk and cloth o' gold,
And London shops are rare shops, where gallant things
   are sold,
And bonnily clinks the gold there, but drowsily blinks the
   eye,
And London Town, of all towns, I'm glad to hurry by.

So hey for the road, the west road, by mill and forge
   and fold,
Scent of the fern and song of the lark by brook, and
   field, and wold.
To the comely folk at the hearth-stone and the talk
   beside the fire,
In the hearty land, where I was bred, my land of heart's
   desire.

John Masefield

THE SWEET O' THE YEAR

THE upland hills are green again;
  The river runs serene again;
    All down the miles
    Of orchard aisles
The pink-lip blooms are seen again;
    To garden close
      And dooryard plot
    Comes back the rose
      And bergamot.

The ardent blue leans near again;
The far-flown swallow is here again;
    To his thorn-bush
    Returns the thrush,
And the painted-wings appear again;
    In young surprise
      The meadows run
    All starry eyes
      To meet the sun.

Warm runs young blood in the veins again,
And warm love floods in the rains again.
    Earth, all aflush
    With the fecund rush,
To her heart's desire attains again;
    While stars outbeat
      The exultant word—
    " Death's in defeat,
      And Love is Lord!"

Charles G. D. Roberts

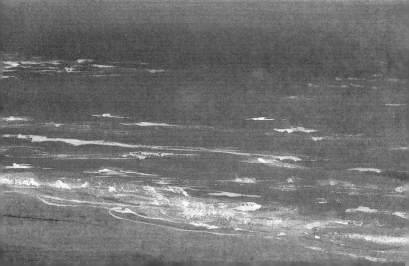

AT DUSK

LEFT to the stars the sky,
    Left to the sea the sand,
Softly the small waves drop
    Hand on white hand:
Where murmuring hills are steep,
Countless musicians keep
    Tryst, among wild, dim valleys
Lost in sleep.

Their music binds a world
    Of alien fields unknown,
Stirs among cloud-hung peaks
    Lovely and lone,
Far and remote they seem,
Playing their endless theme—
    Thin threads of sound come trembling back,
Dream upon dream.

                    Enid Hamilton-Fellows

REVERIE

THE little roads of Lincolnshire
  Will take you anywhere you please,
Perhaps beside a windmill tower,
  Or summer meadow loud with bees;
Sometimes across a humpy bridge,
  Above a slow and reedy stream,
Where there is time to pause awhile,
  And watch the water, half a-dream.

The little roads of Lincolnshire
  Go winding gently up and down,
Through many a sleepy village street,
  Or swallow-haunted market town.
They'll take you to the leafy Wolds,
  Or onward to the shining sea;
And folks will greet you on your way,
  And one of them may well be me.

The little roads of Lincolnshire
  Were made for folks to stop and stare,
To lean upon a weathered gate,
  And breathe the cool, sweet country air.
But if you have to go away,
  Though sad it is to smile and part,
In quiet moments, all alone,
  You'll find them winding through your heart.

Peter Cliffe

ONLY FOUR

MY sister is more big than me
      By half a head or more,
For she is nearly six, you see,
And I am only four.

We play together all day long,
Our play I *do* enjoy,
But she gets rough because she's strong
And I'm a little boy.

She teases me a lot, you know,
And pulls me on the floor
And takes my toys away although
She *knows* I'm only four.

And sometimes when she pushes me
I cry a bit, but then
I am only four, you see,
Just wait till I am ten . . .

                    Sam MacEachan

OF GREATHAM

FOR peace, than knowledge more desirable,
  Into your Sussex quietness I came,
When summer's green and gold and azure fell
  Over the world in flame.

And peace upon your pasture-lands I found,
  While grazing flocks drift on continually,
As little clouds that travel with no sound
  Across a windless sky.

Out of your oaks the birds call to their mates
  That brood among the pines, where hidden
    deep
From curious eyes a world's adventure waits
  In columned choirs of sleep.

Under the calm ascension of the night
  We heard the mellow lapsing and return
Of night-owls purring in their groundling flight
  Through lanes of darkling fern.

Unbroken peace when all the stars were drawn
  Back to their lairs of light, and ranked along
From shire to shire the downs out of the dawn
  Were risen in golden song.

. . . . . .

I sing of peace. Was it but yesterday
  I came among your roses and your corn?
Then momently amid this wrath I pray
  For yesterday reborn.

John Drinkwater

THE SINGING TREE

BENEATH the singing-apple tree,
   My Lady Evening waits for me.
Her dress of blue and lavender,
   Hath wisps of cobweb lace,
I, silver-sandalled, tread with her,
   A sombre, secret place.

And when, in twilight loveliness,
The hills put on a lilac dress,
My Lady Evening glides from me
   Across the silver land,
Then, by the singing-apple tree,
   In loneliness I stand.

The magic apples play for me
A scherzo and a phantasy,
But when the soft night wind doth stray,
   Before the moon is old,
The little leaves and branches play
   A rhapsody in gold.

My little friend, the mottled owl,
Among the scented fruit doth prowl,
And lo, my lady in her flight,
   Hath left a flute for me!
I shall make magic song to-night,
   Beneath the apple tree.

Gloria Rawlinson

THE RIVER RUNS FAST

THE river runs fast
  With the melted snow,
And the green leaves come,
  And the dead leaves go
Hidden in the green grass
  Springing up below.

The white spires of blossom
  On the chestnut trees
Are a-rumble with the wings
  Of the numberless bees,
And the loud birds are back again
  From Southern lands and seas.

The glad days are here now,
  The bright days of sun,
And fast as the river
  The spring days run.
Oh, may I be with you, my love,
  Before the Summer's done!

John Buxton

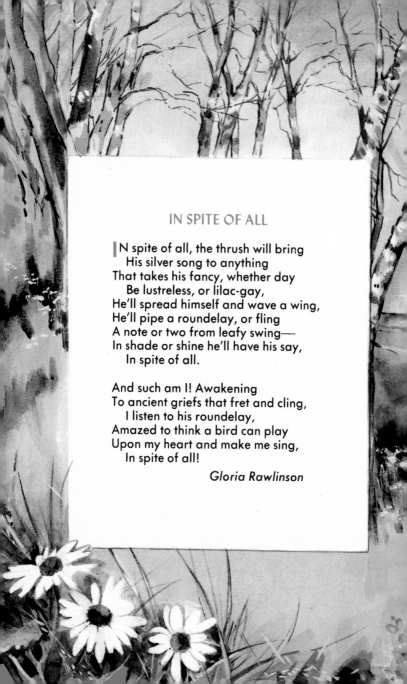

IN SPITE OF ALL

IN spite of all, the thrush will bring
  His silver song to anything
That takes his fancy, whether day
  Be lustreless, or lilac-gay,
He'll spread himself and wave a wing,
He'll pipe a roundelay, or fling
A note or two from leafy swing—
In shade or shine he'll have his say,
  In spite of all.

And such am I! Awakening
To ancient griefs that fret and cling,
  I listen to his roundelay,
Amazed to think a bird can play
Upon my heart and make me sing,
  In spite of all!

Gloria Rawlinson

DOWNLAND RHAPSODY

O GIVE to me the windblown downs
    Away from stuffy streets and towns,
Where skylarks spiral to the sky
O'er tussocked path and thistled rye,
And freckled cowslips nod and smile
Each Springtime, for a little while.

O give to me the rolling downs
In all their softly folded gowns,
Where stencilled steed pricks chalk-lined ears,
And on the slope, forever rears,
Immobile, mute, against the sheen
Of trembling grass and mossy green.

O give to me the changeless downs
With all the greens, the blues, the browns,
Bright butterflies and small wild bees,
Frail harebells bending to the breeze,
And dandelions—past their prime,
Which children pluck to tell the time.

Violet Hall

FARM HORSES

EARLY each morning, past our cottage, come
　　The horses from the farm along the lane:
We listen to the slow and steady drum
　　Of hoofs, and watch them through the window
　　　　pane
As one young lad dismounts beside the gate
　　To open it and let the horses in;
They sniff the air and stamp as if they wait
　　Impatiently for ploughing to begin.

Across the rich, red earth we watch them go,
　　Cleaving long furrows with each gleaming
　　　　blade,
Until by teatime, row on shining row
　　Are ready to be sown. Now are laid
The ploughs aside, and slowly down the lane,
　　Tired with the day, their energy well spent,
We watch them passing homewards once again
　　Back to the farm, to feed and rest content.

Douglas Gibson

DONEGAL COAST

I KNOW that at the end,
   obedient to the sea,
I shall come
to this last utter coast
blinded with light.

All colour gone
but the swift spate of silver,
the grey mountain-shoulder,
wave-commanding,
and my hope in its fastness.

Divided, forsaken,
what should I cling to?
Thought, memory,
the nets of religion
break like a shoal
in the sundering tide-streams.

Here, then, I stand
as night before morning,
the sea at dawn,
and the long waves breaking.
O bright Homeric waters,
I pray you receive me.

Not as a stranger,
not as an outcast,
I come as thy pilgrim,
I call thee to claim me,
by the sands on my feet,
by the salt in my heart.

                    R. N. D. Wilson

AUGUST

NOW is the harvest of the lands
  And painted carts with heavy loads,
Wide as the deep elm-shadowed lanes,
Are drawn by horses with straw-plaited manes
Where the uncut corn still stands
Divided by white dusty roads.

Such peace is here, that tired eyes rest
On green and dust and golden brown
And look no farther than these things.
O quiet as a bird's closed wings
The heart rests, like the eyes. Unguessed
The grain from which its peace has grown.

Ursula Wood

THE RETURN

THE Earth is waiting.
    Waiting for the old, familiar cries
Of birds returning,
    And dropping from the English springtime
    skies.

The house is waiting,
    A muddy patch beneath her empty eaves,
But soon the martins
    Will sport and play amongst her orchard
    leaves.

The folk are waiting,
    To see the swift so elegantly dive,
To hear a cuckoo,
    And know the summer sun will soon arrive.

The wait is over!
    A single swallow swoops above the lane,
His eager chatter
    A welcome part of Summer's sweet refrain.

Susan Benwell